In Step With Nature

HENRY DAVID THOREAU

by Elizabeth Ring

A Gateway Green Biography
The Millbrook Press
Brookfield, Connecticut

For Bill,
great outdoorsman

Cover photo courtesy of The Granger Collection
Background cover photo courtesy of Jim McGrath

Photographs courtesy of: Concord Free Public Library,
Concord, Mass.: p. 4, 7, 10, 35; © Jim McGrath: pp. 13,
30 (bottom); Harvard University Archives, from Baille's
Views of Harvard: p. 16 (top); Bettmann Archives: pp. 16
(bottom), 23; © Bonnie McGrath: pp. 19, 27, 42 (top);
The Pierpont Morgan Library: pp. 21, 42 (bottom); Peter
Arnold: p. 30 (top left: © Jean F. Stoick; top right: ©
Johann Schumacher); Art Resource/National Museum of
American Art, Smithsonian Institution: p. 37.

Library of Congress Cataloging-in-Publication Data

Ring, Elizabeth, 1920-
Henry David Thoreau : in step with nature / Elizabeth Ring.
p.   cm.   (Gateway biography)
Includes bibliographical references and index.
Summary: Introduces the life, thinking, and work of the
New England philosopher and nature writer.
ISBN 1–56294–258–1
1. Thoreau, Henry David, 1817–1862—Biography—Juvenile
literature. 2. Authors, American—19th century—Biography—
Juvenile literature. 3. Naturalists—United States—Biography
—Juvenile literature. [1. Thoreau, Henry David, 1817–1862.
2. Authors, American. 3. Naturalists.]   I. Title   II. Series.
PS3053.R56   1993
818'.309—dc20
[B]   92-11559   CIP   AC

Published by The Millbrook Press
2 Old New Milford Road
Brookfield, Connecticut 06804

Henry David Thoreau

Henry David Thoreau

When *you go outdoors,* you meet nature head on. With no windows or walls between you and the world, you learn to know nature quite well. Winds and breezes swirl past you. Sun, rain, and snow come at you from above. The ground is firm and grassy under your feet.

Nature, in fact, wraps itself all around you. It can get inside you, too. You smell earthy smells. You taste apples and nuts. You hear birds sing loud and clear. You see squirrels, trees, and stars doing what they naturally do. And, when you listen and look hard, nature can tell you an exciting secret or two. It reaches right into your feelings and thoughts.

That is what Henry David Thoreau felt about nature. All his life, in Concord, Massachusetts, he spent more time outdoors than in. When he was a young man, in 1845, he built a small hut by a pond near his home. He lived there for more than two years, having a wonderful time looking around, listening, thinking, and writing things down.

Later, Thoreau wrote a book he called *Walden.* It was his story about living in the woods beside

Walden Pond. This book and Thoreau's other writings have made many people see nature in ways they never saw it before. Thoreau did not plan to become one of the most famous thinkers and nature writers in the world. He just wanted to live his own life and write about it—in his own way.

There were people in the village of Concord who thought Thoreau went his own way much too much from the time he was a small boy. He was too different for them. He did not like parties. He did not attend "sociables" at church. He would rather be out wandering the woods. At times, he would be seen sitting on a log with his nose stuck in a book. When he was grown, the townspeople were not too surprised that he went off to live by himself in a hut in the woods outside town. "Henry always *was* odd," many said.

Henry David Thoreau was born at his grandmother's farmhouse just outside Concord on July 12, 1817. His sister Helen was five when he was born. His brother John was two. His little sister Sophia would come along two years later.

Thoreau's birthplace on Virginia Road in Concord, Massachusetts.

The Thoreaus lived as many New Englanders did in those days. They were good at making do. They worked hard and were thankful for whatever they had. They ate simple, healthy food. The children wore hand-me-down clothes. Henry's were made of plain, sturdy cloth. Although the family owned little, they did not feel poor. In fact, they felt rich. Not everyone in town enjoyed the warm, pleasant family life the Thoreaus did.

Henry's father was a pencilmaker. He was a kind, honest, easygoing man. He loved music and books and he shared this love with his children. Henry learned to play the flute, his sisters the piano. Mr. Thoreau had been a schoolteacher. All his children later taught school at one time or another. He was also a good mechanic and carpenter, an ability he passed along to Henry.

Henry's mother, Cynthia, was always bustling about. She liked to talk a lot. Some people said it was no wonder that Mr. Thoreau was such a quiet man—he had no choice! But Mrs. Thoreau was also known to be good-hearted. She helped others in town, and she took wonderful care of her own family. To earn money she rented rooms in the house to boarders. She was a fine housekeeper and cooked delicious meals.

Henry was closest to his brother John, although the boys were quite different. John loved to be with friends and tell stories and jokes. Henry was quieter and a bit of a loner.

Henry was a strong, thin, brown-haired boy, of medium height for his age. He liked to argue. He could be so solemn that some of his friends called him "Judge." But he could be witty, too. He often had a twinkle in his gray-blue eyes, especially when he was poking fun at something. He never cared much for sports and games, so he was not exactly "one of the gang."

Henry knew he was different. He liked to follow his own heart and head, not anyone else's. Later, he wrote in his journal: "If I do not keep step with others, it is because I hear a different drummer." Ideas were thumping around in Henry's head all the time.

Different as Henry and John were from each other, they got along fine. They never quarreled, not even when, as young men, they fell in love with the same girl. She liked them both but married

*Thoreau was very close to his brother John,
shown in this picture as a young man.*

someone else. No hearts were broken, and they all remained friends.

Neither Henry nor John ever married. Henry thought families were wonderful, and he loved his own and those of his friends. But, he said when he was older, *he* could not have married and had children and, at the same time, lived the life he wanted to live.

Growing up, the boys were together a lot. They often walked along Concord's tree-lined streets. They watched the stagecoaches and ox-carts and farmers' wagons rattle back and forth on the road to Boston, which was 20 miles (32 kilometers) south. They strode past the grocery store, the post office, the bank, the blacksmith shop. Sometimes they ran down to the river to watch big barges plow by.

At home, there were pigs and chickens for the boys to feed, and there were cows to milk and take to pasture. Henry liked animals. He felt that animals—tame or wild—were somehow his "cousins."

Henry also felt related to the Indians that had once lived in the area. He and John played Indians sometimes. They knew where to find old Indian campsites and arrowheads. Henry admired the way Indians respected animals, birds, plants, the sky—all nature.

Concord was a good village to grow up in. It was a famous place. All of the two thousand or so people who lived there were proud of the role Concord had played at the start of the American Revolution. A battle had been fought there almost fifty years before the Thoreaus lived in town. On April 19, 1775, British soldiers had come to Concord to destroy guns and ammunition that were stored there. Hundreds of local minutemen (volunteer soldiers) had fought the British at Concord's old North Bridge. It was one of the first battles for American independence.

Henry and John often walked across the famous wooden bridge. It stood for freedom. One might say the Thoreau boys grew up in Concord with feelings for freedom in their bones.

They both went to Center School, where several grades were taught together in one room. For high school, they went to Concord Academy. They were good, but not great, students.

Both Henry and John were happiest outdoors. Henry, especially, was sure he learned more from

Thoreau often walked across Concord's old North Bridge, where local minutemen once fought for independence from the British.

nature than from school. Walden Pond was one of his favorite places to go. The pond was deep and clear, and so clean you could drink from it. On calm days, you could see the sky reflected in its waters. Some people thought the pond had no bottom. Henry later measured its various depths with a stone on a string. He found it was 102 feet (31 meters) deep at its deepest.

Sometimes Henry would row his boat out to the middle of the pond. He would pull in the oars, lie on his back, look at the sky, and dream. Other times he went fishing. It was great to fish at night under the stars, with a campfire burning on the bank to lure the fish close to shore.

Henry loved books almost as much as he loved nature. When he was sixteen he went to Harvard College in Cambridge, just outside Boston. Harvard later became a huge university, but in 1833 it was a small place with only about 250 students and a few buildings.

Henry spent much of his time in the college library. He read about America, Europe, and Asia.

He became a fine student of Greek. The good education he got at Harvard College showed in the books he later wrote. Henry knew a lot about many things.

One day, Henry discovered the writings of Ralph Waldo Emerson, a Harvard graduate. Emerson's ideas about nature were very much like his own. One of the things Emerson believed was that everyone is a part of the same spirit that is in nature—just as a drop of water is part of an ocean or a sunbeam is part of the sun.

Later, in Concord, Thoreau and Emerson became close friends and shared their ideas. Both wrote down their ideas in their notebooks, both wrote essays and poems, and both gave lectures.

Thoreau graduated from Harvard in 1837, when he was twenty years old. He was glad to get back home. He took a job teaching at Center School, the same grade school he had gone to.

Thoreau liked teaching, but he soon ran into trouble. He was told he must whack students with a ruler when they misbehaved. That was not his way at all. He liked and respected children too much. But the school authorities said it was the

At sixteen, Thoreau went to Harvard College, where he spent a lot of time in the library.

Ralph Waldo Emerson, whose ideas about nature were much like Thoreau's.

only way to keep children from becoming spoiled. Thoreau did not believe that. So, two weeks after he started teaching, he quit Center School.

The following year, Henry and his brother John started a school of their own in Concord, in the buildings of Concord Academy. They ran things their way. After regular classes, Henry and John would often take students swimming or sailing on the river. Or they would hike through the woods and look for Indian arrowheads. These outings were not just for fun. Students were learning first-hand about animals, Indians, geography, biology, plant life, and history.

These outdoor trips were the best way in the world to learn about ecology (although few people used that word then). The children could easily see for themselves how plants and animals need their special places, or habitats, in order to survive: Swamp plants cannot grow on hilltops; forest birds need seeds and insects to eat and trees to nest in. The Thoreaus' students learned how important it is to protect the earth's environment so that plants and creatures can live in their proper places.

The school had rules, of course, but students

who misbehaved were never hit with a ruler. One visitor to the school said he had never seen such well-behaved students having such a good time at their lessons. More and more students came. But in 1841, less than three years after the school opened, John became ill. He probably had tuberculosis, a serious lung disease. He could not teach anymore, and the school had to be closed. It was a big disappointment to everyone. The Thoreau brothers' teaching methods were so respected that they were later used in other schools.

Out of a job again, Henry went to work in his father's pencil shop. He never really liked the dusty pencil business, but off and on throughout his life he helped out at the little factory. He even found a way to make much better pencils. That made the business more successful, and the whole Thoreau family was much better off. But even though he enjoyed the success, Henry's heart was not in pencil making. He would much rather study nature and write

In fact, next to tramping through the woods or reading books, Henry Thoreau liked most to write. He wrote in his journal almost every day. He kept

Thoreau and his brother started their own school in Concord and often took students swimming or sailing on the river there.

notes on all kinds of things he saw, things he did, things he read, and things he just thought about. He liked to write poems, too.

In the fall of 1839, Henry and John went on a two-week boat trip. Henry wrote about the trip in his journal. He told how they went down the Concord River, through canals, and up the Merrimack River and back. They had a fine time rowing, sailing, camping, hiking, swimming, watching animals, examining plants, and talking with river boatmen.

It was a trip Henry would always remember. Less than three years later, in January 1842, John suddenly died. He was only twenty-seven years old. He did not die of the lung disease that had made him sick. He had an accident. One day he cut his finger with a razor. It was just a small cut and he paid little attention to it. But an infection called tetanus set in and caused his death.

Henry was sick with sadness at his brother's death. Only when spring came did he begin to feel better. Then he got outdoors more. He played his flute again. After a while, nature and music helped cure Henry's sadness at losing John.

For most of his life, Thoreau kept a journal
of his adventures and observations.

Henry *went back* to work, taking jobs around town as a handyman. He was an expert carpenter and fixer of things and a good gardener, too. He learned how to survey land, and he earned money measuring acres of farms and miles of rivers and roadways. He worked to earn just enough to live on because he wanted to have time to do the things he really loved to do. He believed all his life that most people worked much too hard just so that they could buy things they did not need.

Some days, Thoreau worked at Ralph Waldo Emerson's house. Then Emerson invited Thoreau to live in his big white house on Lexington Road. Thoreau had his own room there. He was good friends with Emerson's wife, Lidian, and the small Emerson children.

After two years there, Thoreau went to Staten Island, New York, where he taught Emerson's three nephews for a short while. While he was living on Staten Island, he visited New York City. Other people, like the poet Walt Whitman, loved New York. But Thoreau did not. All that noise! All those horses and carriages up and down Broadway,

*Ralph Waldo Emerson's large white house
on Lexington Road in Concord. For two years,
Thoreau had his own room there.*

a rumbling wooden street! Grunting pigs rooted for garbage in dirty alleys. He did, however, like the bookstores, art galleries, and theaters. And he did meet a few fine people. The great newspaper editor, Horace Greeley, was one. Greeley later helped Thoreau publish some of his writings. But after just a few months Henry was homesick, and back to Concord he went.

Thoreau moved back home with his parents. Again he worked in the pencil factory. He often visited Emerson. He could always find good company there. Sometimes it would be the writer Nathaniel Hawthorne, who also lived in Concord. By now, Ralph Waldo Emerson was known as an important thinker and writer. He gave lectures everywhere. Philosophers, poets, and writers from England and other parts of Europe came to see him. Many shared Emerson's interest in Eastern philosophies.

Emerson and many of his friends had some big ideas to talk about. They discussed what the "real world" was all about. Things we see, hear, touch, smell, and taste, they said, are signs or symbols of the world of the spirit.

We get to know this world of the spirit, they said, by getting to know nature. A flower, for instance, might tell us about the spirit of beauty. A rock might give us the idea of strength.

We cannot see, hear, touch, taste, or smell beauty and strength as we can a flower or a rock. But by being close to nature, we can get a hint of the spirit that *transcends* (is above) material things. All we have to do is get away from useless, routine activities, go outdoors, and listen to nature as it speaks to us.

Many people in Concord—and elsewhere— found such ideas pretty hard to understand. They thought these *transcendentalists* (as the thinkers called themselves) must be walking around with their heads in the clouds! A flower is a flower, they said. A rock is a rock. Period.

But many other people liked the thought that all people and things in this world are part of one good, wise, gentle spirit. Thoreau himself lived by these ideals. But being Henry Thoreau, he never formally joined the groups that many of these thinkers formed. He just lived his ideals in his own way.

In the spring of 1845, Thoreau was twenty-seven years old. He was ready to do some serious writing. Up until then, he had written articles and essays, and notes in his journal. Now he had something more ambitious in mind—a book.

But first he needed a quiet place to think and write. Emerson owned some woodsy land by Walden Pond, just a mile or two out of town. Would he give Henry permission to build a small hut there? Yes, he would.

Thoreau borrowed an ax and cut down some pine trees. Then he dug a hole for a cellar. After making a stone foundation, Thoreau started to build. He liked the idea of building his own home. He wanted to construct it as simply and snugly as a bird builds its nest.

He ended up with a cozy little house a bit bigger than a toolshed. To be exact, Henry's new home measured 10 feet wide by 15 feet long by 8 feet high (3 by 4.5 by 2.5 meters). He later put in a fireplace and built a woodshed. The hut cost him exactly $28.12½ to build. He furnished the cabin with a bed, a table, a desk, three chairs, a few pots

A replica of the small house that Thoreau built on Walden Pond. Thoreau lived there by himself for two years and two months.

and pans, some writing materials, and other things he really needed.

Thoreau moved into his hut on the Fourth of July, 1845, Independence Day for America—and for him too, in a way. At least, he must have felt fancy free, removed from all the everyday hustle and bustle. He planned to find out how a person could live simply—and be happy at the same time.

"I went to the woods," he wrote later, in his book *Walden*, "because I wished to . . . see if I could not learn what it had to teach, and not, when I came to die, discover that I had not lived."

Every day he got up early. Some things he *had* to do, such as chop wood for his fire or hoe the big bean field he had planted. Other parts of his days were full of surprises as he came face-to-face with the unspoiled nature around him.

Most of the time, he did indeed live simply. He ate potatoes and corn that he raised. He traded beans for sugar and rice. He often dined on fish he caught and wild plants he found.

While he was at Walden, Thoreau was alone a good deal. But he was never lonely. When he did want company, he walked into town and had dinner with family or friends. He was, he admitted, "naturally no hermit." Some weeks he went to Concord every day.

Visitors came to the hut now and then, too. There were many good talks there or in the shade of the pines nearby. Thoreau had animal neighbors to keep him company, too. One mouse built its nest in his cellar. It was so tame it ate cheese from Thoreau's hand.

Birds lived close by. A phoebe built a nest in the shed. A robin built one in a pine tree next to the house. One of Thoreau's favorite wild visitors was a loon. The big black bird came to the pond in the fall. Its "wild laughter" (more like a wolf than a bird, he wrote) would often wake Thoreau up in the morning.

One afternoon, the loon and Thoreau played a game of tag all over the pond. The loon dived. Thoreau, madly paddling his boat, chased it. He tried to guess where the loon, speeding underwater like a fish, would come up next. He never guessed right. The loon popped up far off and laughed at him. At least it seemed that way to Thoreau. He had to laugh, too.

One of Thoreau's favorite wild visitors at Walden Pond was a loon (left) that played a game of tag with him. Birds and animals lived close to Thoreau. A phoebe (right) even built a nest in his hut.

The winter months on Walden Pond often found Thoreau writing at his desk before the cabin fire.

In winter, there were hours to spend writing. Snows came and stayed. Thoreau, snug in his cabin, sat at his desk before his fire and wrote page after page. From the notes in his journal, he wrote the story of the wonderful trip he and John had taken on the Concord and Merrimack rivers.

When spring came to Walden Pond, Thoreau was outdoors again much of the time. He saw things come alive. Woodland plants turned green. Birds started nesting. The world was waking up after its long winter sleep.

He watched the snow melt and make patterns in the mud and sand. Little streams of water looked to him like leaves, vines, birds' feet, or veins under one's own skin. What he saw made him think again how much people are part of nature. Spring, he said, is a good time for us all to "turn over a new leaf," to wake up, to start a new life.

Thoreau was so happy at Walden Pond, you might think that he would want to stay there in his hut forever. But in September of 1847, after two years and two months, he decided to leave. He had wondered what he would learn by living close to nature day after day. Now he felt wiser, richer, and stronger. He had wondered if he could live both simply and happily. He found out that he could.

"I left the woods," Thoreau said, "for as good a reason as I went there. Perhaps it seemed to me that I had several more lives to live, and could not spare any more time for that one."

Many Concord folks welcomed their neighbor back home, but not everyone. Thoreau might have changed, but his critics had not. Many people would never understand what this "wild-looking, crusty, selfish, lazy woodsman" (as they saw him) was up to.

Several people, for instance, wanted to talk about the day he went to jail for not paying his taxes. What kind of citizen refused to pay taxes? they asked.

What they said was true. Henry had not paid his poll tax and one day, while on a trip to town from his hut, he had been arrested and had spent a night in jail. But he felt he had a good reason for not paying taxes. For three years, he had refused to give his money ($1.50 each year) to a government that was, for one thing, helping slaveowners keep slaves. He knew for certain that slavery was wrong. He and many other local people had helped runaway slaves escape to Canada. (Several Concord people continued to do so until the Civil War ended slavery once and for all in 1865).

Besides, the government was spending tax money to fight a war with Mexico. Thoreau didn't want his tax money paying for that. But the town constable said he was setting a bad example for other taxpayers, and Thoreau was jailed overnight. Someone (he never knew who) paid his fine and Thoreau was quickly freed.

Later, Thoreau gave a lecture about refusing to pay taxes titled "On the Relation of the Individual to the State." The talk was later called "Resistance to Civil Government." Widely published, it is known today as *Civil Disobedience.* In it, he said there are good laws and bad laws. He was all for obeying good laws. But, he said, he believed there are times when you can disobey the government and obey the "higher laws" of your own conscience. You just have to be willing to pay the price—as he did in going to jail. He asked: "Is it not possible that an individual can be right and a government wrong?" Many people all over the world—in Russia, India, and here in the United States—have been inspired by his words to challenge laws that they have believed to be unjust.

The year after he left Walden Pond, Thoreau took care of the Emerson home and family while Emerson was in Europe. The children were delighted to have him back. They loved the way he told stories and popped corn with them at the fireplace.

When Emerson came home, Thoreau moved into a new house he had helped his father build for the family on Main Street. He furnished his attic room with the bed, desk, and chairs from his hut. It was a quiet place where he wrote—mostly in the evenings. In the mornings he worked at some job or other for pay, and in the afternoons he still roamed the Concord woods, fields, and swamps. He often carried a spyglass or a microscope with him. He invented a hat that would hold small plants and animals to take home to examine more closely.

Thoreau furnished his attic room in the family house on Main Street, Concord, with the bed, desk, and chairs from his Walden Pond cabin.

Thoreau studied nature very carefully. But he did not think of himself as a scientist or a naturalist. He felt more like a poet of nature. He was more interested in what nature *meant* than what it *was* scientifically. Even so, scientists have often read his work to find out exactly how certain animals behave or how certain plants grow.

Over the next few years, Thoreau made several short trips away from Concord. He visited Cape Cod, Maine (three times), Vermont, New Hampshire, New York State, and Canada. Maine was his favorite place because parts of it were so wild and unspoiled. He climbed mountains, rode river rapids, and with an Indian guide saw moose and other wildlife he would not have found around home. One of America's first conservationists, Thoreau believed that parts of the country should remain wild. How else would people know what unspoiled nature was truly like?

His first book, *A Week on the Concord and Merrimack Rivers,* was published in 1849, but only a few copies were sold. Thoreau had to buy over

Thoreau loved the unspoiled beauty of Maine, captured here in "High Cliff, Coast of Maine" by Winslow Homer.

seven hundred copies back from the publisher. So be it, he said. Actually, he rather liked not being well known. He had more privacy to go on writing and enjoying nature.

In writing *Walden,* Thoreau told about his two years in the woods as if everything happened within one year. The story is not meant to be plain fact; it is partly fact and partly fancy. It is beautiful, wise, at times cranky, and often good fun. The whole book adds up to what Thoreau saw as the truth about life.

By the time Thoreau turned forty years old, in 1857, he was feeling old, he said. He was wearing false teeth. He had been sick off and on. He got colds and infections so easily he wore a long beard to help keep his throat warm.

But he was in good spirits. He kept exploring the woods and fields. Walking at night became a special treat, finding his way like an animal in the dark. He went on short visits to New York State and New Hampshire. When his father died in 1859, Thoreau took charge of the pencil business with the help of his sister Sophia. He also gave lectures, and he always kept writing.

Because he got colds easily, Thoreau wore
a long beard to keep his throat warm.

Then, one cold, wet December day in 1860, he came home from a walk having caught a bad cold. The cold got worse. He was, in fact, suffering from tuberculosis. John had probably been ill with the same lung disease, and his sister Helen is thought to have died of it in 1849.

When Thoreau heard that the cold climate in Minnesota might help him, he went there. But he came home feeling worse than ever. Slowly he weakened. After a while, he could speak only in a whisper. He knew he was dying, but he did not feel sad. He had led the rich, simple life he had wanted to lead, and he had written about it.

Once, he wrote: "If you have built castles in the air . . . that is where they should be. Now put foundations under them." He himself had dreamed dreams and then brought them to life.

"My life," he said, "has been the poem I would have writ." He actually felt happy, as if he were "changing," he said, rather than dying.

Thoreau died peacefully on May 6, 1862. He was forty-four years old. His last words were "moose" and "Indian." That might have meant that, in his mind, he was on his way back to Maine.

Thoreau was buried in the family plot in Sleepy Hollow Cemetery in Concord, beside his brother John. One word is carved on his gravestone: Henry.

Although Thoreau was not famous while he was alive, his book, *Walden,* sold steadily after he died. So, later, did *Civil Disobedience* and *A Week on the Concord and Merrimack Rivers.* His fame grew even greater as other books (taken from his own notes) were published: *Excursions, The Maine Woods, Cape Cod, A Yankee in Canada,* and other parts of the *Journal* itself.

Henry Thoreau is gone. But as the world becomes more and more complex, people continue to find deeper meaning in his books. His words lift the spirits of those who wish to lead good, full, simple lives.

Walden Pond remains. It is as clear as it always was, but the surroundings have changed. Emerson's heirs left their pond and surrounding property to the public, so that others could enjoy its beauty. There is a park there now. That might have pleased Thoreau. He once said that every town and city should have a park or woodland to go to for quiet and peace.

Thoreau's simple gravestone in Concord.

The front flyleaf inscription in one of Thoreau's many journals.

Today, some visitors go to the pond to picnic or swim. There is a public beach across the pond from where Thoreau built his hut. Some people have not cared about the land and have not treated it well. That would certainly make Thoreau snort in disgust—and probably write a scolding essay or two.

But many people go to the pond to be inspired by the beauty Thoreau saw there. These people want to preserve the park the way they know Thoreau would like it to be forever.

You can visit the park. You can go to the very spot where the famous hut once stood. You can sit where Thoreau's doorway used to be, look at the pond through the trees, and dream. The foundation stones are still there. All you have to do is use your imagination to rebuild his hut—or build your own "castle"—in the air.

Important Dates

1817	Born July 12 in Concord, Massachusetts.
1823–1833	Attends Center School and Concord Academy.
1833–1837	Attends Harvard College. Starts his *Journal*.
1838–1841	Operates a private school with brother John.
1839	Goes on boating trip with John on the Concord and Merrimack rivers.
1841	Goes to live with the Emerson family.
1842	His brother John dies.
1843	Invents a better way to make pencils. Visits New York City.
1845	Moves into his hut at Walden Pond on July 4.
1846	Spends a night in jail for not paying his taxes.
1847	Leaves Walden Pond on September 6.
1848	Gives a lecture on "Civil Disobedience."
1849	*A Week on the Concord and Merrimack Rivers* is published.
1854	*Walden* is published.
1862	Dies on May 6 at age forty-four.

Further Reading

About Henry David Thoreau

Henry David Thoreau, A Man For Our Time, by James Daugherty (Viking, 1967)

Henry David Thoreau, by Douglas Miller (Facts on File, 1991)

Henry David Thoreau, A Neighbor to Nature, by Catherine Reef (Twenty-First Century Books, Henry Holt, 1991)

A Man Named Thoreau, by Robert Burleigh (Atheneum, 1985)

The Night Thoreau Spent in Jail, by Jerome Lawrence and Robert E. Lee (Bantam, 1983)

Thoreau, As Remembered by a Young Friend, by Edward Waldo Emerson (Houghton Mifflin, 1917)

By Henry David Thoreau

The Indians of Thoreau, Selections from the Indian Notebooks (Hummingbird, 1974)

Walden (abridged edition) (The Peter Pauper Press, 1966)

Walden and Other Writings of Henry David Thoreau (The Modern Library, Random House, 1981)

A Week on the Concord and Merrimack Rivers (Parnassus Imprints, 1987)

Index